Collecting Stars
from a
Night's Sky

Collecting Stars from a Night's Sky

poems by
Oppong Clifford Benjamin

Poetic Justice Books & Arts
Port Saint Lucie, Florida

©2019 Oppong Clifford Benjamin

book design and layout: SpiNDec, Port Saint Lucie, FL
cover design: Kris Haggblom

All rights reserved.

No part of this book may be used or reproduced in any manner whatsoever without written permission except in the case of brief quotations embodied in critical articles and reviews. Members of educational institutions and organizations wishing to photocopy any of the work for classroom use, or authors, artists and publishers who would like to obtain permission for any material in the work, should contact the publisher.

Published by Poetic Justice Books
Port Saint Lucie, Florida
www.poeticjusticebooks.com

ISBN: 978-1-950433-18-6

FIRST EDITION
10 9 8 7 6 5 4 3 2 1

Collecting Stars from a Night's Sky

a mother teaches her daughter how to marry 3
the storm is upon you 4
class 3 printing fee 5
sanity is (in)sanity 8
the geographical sperm 10
i'm thinking of shapes 11
we're called humans 12
the thing about this place 13
i grew around this table 14
an applause for my mum 15
faith, fate and fear 16
lucifer 17
patience and industry 18
love wrapped in a brown paper 19
the conversation 20
oration 21
my uniform love 22
strandbad eldena 23
the unburnt 24
romantic nonsense 25
stained white sheets 26
don't push it 27
the thing around the waist of a woman 28
for bastards who knew more 29
silent murderer 30
mrs. grace nartey 31
erosion 33
leaving must mean l.e.a.v.i.n.g 34
13 nights of sex before hell 35
tomorrow is coming 36
when she cums, she comes to her senses 37
you have poetry stuck in your throat 38
smoke, words and cups 39
pride 40

mystical love 41
why we are full of shit, women 43
roman conversation 44
no shame rapist 45
how much is life? 46
be gone 47
the power of the female skin 48
wells of our fathers 49
my son, i lied 51
my lame friend 52
faustina ama dadson 54
hello mirror 55
nothing like a friend 56
when they say your best is not enough 57
clementine and her john 58

about the author 61

Collecting Stars
from a
Night's Sky

a mother teaches her daughter how to marry

a lazy chair.
a record player.

                be in a white bridal gown   be beautiful for the mirror

          sunflower with a piece of sun   hold it dear to your breast.

                                          red candles bring the best in marriages
                                                      light five, at least
                                                 place them before the mirror.

              a bottle of champagne, one bottle of red wine brewed in south africa

look at you, be surprised and yell   oh! my! god! i'm beautiful, and respond yes, you are.

            look again at the mirror keenly, your husband is in white gown too
         say yes i do. say you may kiss your groom. throw sunflower over your head
                              veer to catch your flower and smile.
                     tongue to tongue, kiss your husband
              don't let go your only chance of true love
                          hug him tight
               the mirror will break down in your hands
        sharp edges may slice up your flesh and blood may ooze-
           the breaking of your hymen. honeymoon is here, enjoy!

eat three steps back. play soft music to thin the air.
pop champagne and make merry and shout sporadically.
feel free to think you are doing the wrong thing
and collapse your doubts into a lazy chair
with the bottle in the right and wine glass in your left
god is watching, but pretend you are alone and bless your marriage
read the label prayerfully
clos malverne
a pinotage from the stellenbosch wine region.

and that's the ceremony of sologamy. marry yourself before anybody else does.

the storm is upon you

you wake up to
a storm passing through your veranda
you're heavy like a piece of wood in the waters.
your lover calls your name across his room.
he calls you freedom
and you remember you were a bird only yesterday
there's no response from the threshold of the storm.
he calls you heat
and you smile like wildfire.
yesterday the wind came and left it shadow
under your matrimonial bed
where lost panties of all the girls in your church are found.
he lies. he has too many lies about himself than the taste
   of lipsticks on his tongue.
he coils around your neck to sniff the perfume on your body
you smell like water. wait!
you taste even like cocaine, he rustles without shame
your lover's tongue was employed in laying the bricks
of the temple
wherein women go when they let go.
when marriages become storms in verandas
it is legal to shut your door
to avoid drowning or being washed away.

class 3 printing fee

he stood in a tired uniform
well ironed and tucked
and his shorts fusiform
today was exams day and he couldn't wait to write

he walked to his mum for the usual morning blessings
she tried to tell him that he probably should stay home
he bowed his head and she threw her eyes away
they both knew why it was best to stay

but he knew what to say
what to tell his teacher's cane and his mates who might
   laugh again
of why he will write but can't pay

his mother knew it would be another day when her second child
will end education and chase after life around the traffic light
she sensed the aroma of history repeating itself today
and tried harder to keep him at home
but the little boy went to school
ready to tell all about why he will write but can't pay

they were many kids seated in arranged rows and columns
he saw the blank desk. it was obvious kweku wouldn't come
one by one, the teacher inspected their printing-fee receipts
some showed a full year, others for the term...
and he sat there, hoping to do magic

at last the teacher got to his desk
every child was watching with their faces covered with laughs
it was an old story: he would be thrown out again
show me your receipt, the teacher requested
if you don't have to go home, a boy retorted

no printing fee, no exams, another dared to shout
...and now, they all teased

i'm sorry you will have to go home, said the teacher
he stood up, opened his mouth as if to cry then shut it
go on, do you have anything to say? teacher urged

in tears, he closed his eyes, clapped both palms together
and like a humble prayer, he said:

i don't want to be like kwabena, my elder brother
who lost his education on a day like this
his daily bread is now oven by the red light on the street

i don't want my mother to keep wishing for graduates
yet crying for the fact that she can't afford one
i don't want any of my mates here to think me dumb
because i have not the chance to prove myself

don't talk of my father, he is long resting and heaven is far
   away from here
he too had a task for me: become an engineer
please, sir, allow me education and one day we both won't regret

this minute, you are deleting a future
this minute, you can create a destiny
this minute break the rules to make an engineer and heaven will smile.
this is my humble plea

he opened his eyes to his ultimate dismay
every eye was flooding
the teary teacher apologized and promised him his help

later at home, his mum
took the exams question paper
in a gentle voice, she asked, how did you do it?

now he is a civil engineer
an award-winning poet
...and the author of this particular piece

sanity is (in)sanity

the caller said 'madam',
a happy silence hanged in the caller's throat 'you can pick
   your son at 11 am'.
a mother drives an suv
into a mental hospital.
the wind hid the glory of god in empty leaves
it was a sunny day's 2 pm
under a mighty hospital tree,
the son sat under its shade
he gazed at everything that was nothing
he left his face in the hospital
and hid whatever remained of a proud son in his shirt
as if shielding the wind and the leaves against telling him god existed
but he really hid his body so that
his face wouldn't be the first thing
his mother will see in the parkway.
he had given up on religion
but he pretended to bear the cross around his neck.

what do you call mothers who have cried too many times
   about their sons?
he is sick, a mother weeps
he is behind police bars, a mother weeps
he is bipolar, a mother weeps
he is in an asylum for depression, a mother weeps even the more.
'i'm tired! i'm just tired
now i want to say i give up on you'
tears played on her contoured cheeks,
she kicked the leaves and allowed the wind to return them to nature
she wished she could just kick her proud son to death
after all, death is the reservoir of nature
it houses us all till eternity comes for us.
the boy began to recreate his face in the mirror

a new car? nice!
as if he knew she wouldn't answer him.

the world sat in the car with them
she parked at a roadside to seek answers
'what is the cause of your recurring depression...what do you need?'
everyone in the world screamed at once
'answer me because i've given up on you and i'm about to give
   up on life too'
the world is unfair not to have a name for this moment
where a mother seeks life in his son's face,
but the face is everything death left with men

depressions are scars on bodies
always hidden under clothes
no one will see that your son is depressed
i promise not to embarrass you in public
i will just not respond to greetings
i will like to be quiet
i like my space
that way we make life beautiful.
loving nature is loving the flow of days
and everything days come with.
let depression just flow with time
let it go with the oceans
and let it find us again at the river banks,
with time, it will flow again.
one craft we've mastered is how to swim through storms.

the geographical sperm

with pieces of her smile scattered everywhere on the chair,
my mother told me she knew the world map more than i did
and a fat smirk grew in my soft cheeks.
in truth, laughter hid in my teeth.
her words leaked off her stroke-stricken mouth as
she said: nigeria is located behind your husband's voice.
silence!
thoughts ran freely
cute silence stood in my body.
like lightning in a cloudy sky, a young smile brushed my
   mother's teeth.
look here, she managed
last night when your husband spoke, a slum in lagos came in mind
where a walk to the mosque means a walk through people's bedrooms,
and to the marketplace, an experience in adewuni brothel
where careless sperms are lost forever.
in sex, your husband has traveled the world and back.
her face turned into a forest of winter trees
when she said: but israel is very close to nigeria.
and yet she insisted she wasn't telling a war story.

i'm thinking of shapes

the shape of a sea is a ship
carrying bodies of frightened boys
to where they can kiss boys
without having to run into obituary posters on lagos walls.

the shape of hope
is a wooden cabin of the ship
with a window
to remind the boys of stories
their foreign lovers told them
about boys who wore their skin
like it's the only cloth they will ever own.
they've become a part of the breeze,
part of the beautiful things freedom brings in harvard. in
   cambridge, massachusetts.
and the sea below them
has taken the shape of distant faces
who waits on time to afford them this voyage.

i guess the shape of patience
is always late but worth the wait.

we're called humans

a boy tells his lover in six languages
he understands that he is
the long empty street he will
walk as a therapy for insanity.

we are the flowers with yellows
to be busy is to love somebody
so step into the earth, tear off a petal
and pretend you are growing.
forget about life and its twin
forget about time
draw a circle with your breath.
we wonder what we can do
when we look at the woman
shutting the last door in her eyes
she said death can come, she gives up
but we are just the monkeys who fell off the tree, we were trying to fly
we want to believe the butterflies
are our friends.
but butterflies just love to feed on yellows.
and the flow of water on a woman's body is humans
praying to shapeless faces of deities.

the thing about this place

boys at this place wake up in the middle of our prayers to plant misery in our hearts.

they become characters of the stories beneath our mother's tongue. they raise their hands simultaneously in a night's dance among things that dance at nights.

i've learnt to hold together all harsh touches in between my thighs whenever i use the pavements. i close my eyes and pretend to be here and happy. at least, that's the shape of survival at this place. that's how a girl endures slap, her clothes torn apart and dragged on concrete pavements. the one thing mothers tell their daughters to remember of this place is the darkness of sky which always betray its victims.

most often, i imagine my brother and i cum.

these boys have no sundays in their world just like they have no shame carrying their manhood on their shoulders at night.

and in the morning, i swear that you will be greeted in smiles. school boys will smile at you as if saying you did well yesterday night. street gangs with sticks of cigarette in their teeth will mix your name with smoke as if your name suddenly became holy

then they wash you down their throats with guinness beer.

i grew around this table

our dining table round
it brings us around and bound
seats not far from the centre reach
six beautiful chairs, one for each
a tablecloth to cover and adorn
it was colourful though one side torn
our dining table smooth veneer
carefully protected at least for a year
red rose flower in the middle placed
dad and mum sat opposite faced
on the plateau of our dining table
showed daddy's pocket was stable
sugar, milk, milo, bread, custard
butter, fruits, peanuts and salad
we ate well and lived well
watched cartoons of robinson wood
we grew faster and soon were old
then we saw everything go cold
first to vanish from our table was custard
sarah didn't like it, she became blustered
dad said our school fees had gone high
so mum compensated with our chicken thigh
as days passed, so did our salad and fruits
no more cartoons, tv showed a man with his flute
we grew older to a naked table
which was ripped off its cloth
we saw how the family became unstable
our dinning table's veneer destroyed by moth
so today it's packed backyard.

an applause for my mum

just a single room back in the days
no light, television, you said patience pays
one fat mattress, one huge alata blanket
one corner of same room, utensils packed in a basket
another corner, three ghana-must-go bags
behind the door, a hill of dirty rags
until you stayed with us in the rainy seasons
you wouldn't know their use and the reasons
if the rains came in the afternoon
when no one at home, our room, a lagoon
if a relative visits, mum shared the bed
we slept on bare floor with books to support our head
war befell the one who didn't wake up at six
insults, anger, canes and on lucky days kicks
unless brother mic, the pharmacist down the street
confirms you are ill and needs more rest to treat
those sundays mum sat on the last pew
in her heart were many but in hands few
the body was willing to serve but the pocket weak
yet she never stayed home, worshipping every week
can we applaud and dance
to the rhymes of the future?

faith, fate and fear

a man must hold the hand of another to survive religion.
the atmosphere chases the air into wind
just the same way men go back into wombs.
god doesn't take lives, rather humans give their lives to god.

jim said religion is synonymous with fear.
the last time he saw a thief being chased,
he laughed out loud, held his stomach
and shouted he is too religious to die.
he needs a hand to direct him to light. he is thirsty.

a prisoner wears a white cassock,
throws incense on other inmates
and when jim dared to break the bars,
the prisoners said words and stones will not break their
  souls from faith.

the line separating fate and faith
is a lanky man in a white cassock
with incense in hand and spreading fear
and not death nor condemnation to hellfire.

lucifer

i thought men ruined hidden cathedrals under the breasts of women.
then i met him
handsome, gentle.
maybe not all men
come with the maul
nor the sledge in their words.
i assured myself i was in heaven
drinking wine and loving another man sent from god
his words were songs
and listening to him
meant laying with a naked tide
of a virgin sea.
of course, he always
had his words
with him
and he discovered that
the flesh in between my thighs
was a rich ore hidden in earth.
with his words alone, he mined gold till i became dust.
i should have known lucifer was a gentleman.

patience and industry

i know the names
of the boys who go fishing
in the sea every dawn.
they wait for what they cannot see
and hope that at the rise of their nets
at sunset
plenty would come with a smile
and they can share a song
at the beautiful side of a day's
twilight.
there's a style they sit on their canoes
under the scorching sun
their dry faces telling stories of patience
to the waters
holding on to their industry with zeal
and waiting for nothing yet all they prayed for
they know all about fishing -
patience and industry.

love wrapped in a brown paper

how do you
love a man
like me
who searches for
another woman
in your eyes
when he looks
at you and smile

it is the holy places
she took me to that
my tongue finds
whenever i tell you to
spread wide your legs
my tongue recites
holy rosary which prays
to her name instead.

you still love her, you asked
and i looked away
avoiding the tears
in your eyes.
but like the guilt in my heart
those tears find
a way to tell me you'll be here
you'll love until you're loved.

the conversation

i'm in a dark room with a teenager after a heavy rainfall.
it is 11:42 pm.
we are measuring life. and he is telling me
to reach,
you must walk back to the womb of your mother,
to where it all began. return to yourself.
strength grows in that part of the sea
where boys cast their nets and say
we will try again.
who else apart from you knows your name?
who knows how high you go when you give up?
cry when you have earned tears. and laugh when you share a beer.
be proud you fall like a lizard.
hurt your belly. nod. and run.
your race ends at where you began.
run into your body. run into yourself.
life is a race against yourself.

oration

at the edge of the end,
when darkness finally rules over light
before i also fall,
i will say a prayer:
may it be that even when darkness
directs the world to depths of oceans,
you will swim to land
you will find your path.
may it be that by your fire
the world may glow again.
you're what you don't even know,
a supernatural being
a mystery is locked inside you.
a shadow grows on you
a tall, thick shadow
in the form of storms
in the shape of everything
that resembles evil
is eating up the whole world
but may it be that you will be the
only thing to rescue the sun,
to see the face of light again.
and finally,
may you be a wiser adam
when you are here alone.

my uniform love

air in a room cold
hair on my skin fold
where my lover go?
shy, almost timid is
my lover of yesterday.
ajar my door
peep in, my lover
my naked body lay.
my lover of an honourable profession
my heart, stab
and
from a height, i fall
in love i am dead
happy death!
wake me not, ye friends
who laugh across your shoulders
your hands at my ejaculation clap
while my own in my lover i sow.
my lover of an honourable profession
my lover of uniform green
you know ghosts as you know your babies
kill me again when i wake tomorrow
in love, i want to dead remain.

strandbad eldena

to speak the language of the people
is to speak to their sea.

living on the strandbad eldena beach
i could hear the voices of all the germans i have ever known

their faces reach out to mine
inelastic smiles.
i almost laughed. i almost choked.

god was there and never here.
i tell you that
the face of god is found in the voices of playful children screaming
    in the sea
found in the nakedness of sweet ladies rolling on the white sands.

and i knew the word love
is synonymous with a black boy
who admires the white boys
who wear their swimsuits in a way that say
fuck! the world is a lot better when everyone is having sex

history resides in the religious books that read
you have never been to greifswald
if you have not visited the strandbad sea.

the unburnt

no wife slams the door behind her
unless her body is burning inside her husband's words.
her beauty no longer exists in the eyes of he beholder.
there's a home behind slammed doors
where wives go down in ashes, bathe in tears
and they allow the waters to wash away their love,
where they try something like sitting
like bargaining for breath. they sigh and sneeze.
on concrete floors behind the slammed door
a womanizer's wife waits on time
to call her by the first of her names:
the unburnt.

romantic nonsense

people are scared of your silence.

i saw how fears brought tears to your lover's eyes
when he asked you: why won't you complain?
his voice was the face
of kids supporting the losing team
in a stadium
his heart raced through rains
that fell like half-bitten apples
his thick lips waggled in silver waters
when he said: your silence kills.
i swear i could tell he was a dead leaf
somersaulting in the air and wandering on earth to locate hell.
but you wore your secrets in your teeth
your next actions were in the open of your skin
and your words were obvious: i'm fine.
there is pain in waiting and it hurts most
when you're waiting for the end to start.

you watched him eat his soul up and lick his fingers
he tried to know your next set of words
as your lips danced his hopes to grave: i'm fine.
i need to visit the washroom, he said
you laughed softly and kissed his lips
you hugged his imperfect body
he changed into liquid and evaporated away.
your lover is now the lipstick you wear on your lips
to kiss any other man. men say you taste bitter like death.
at least, he could have prompted you to be human too.

stained white sheets

a philanderer's wife performed a strange magic last night.
she turned a paper certificate into a ceramic cup of coffee.
she pulled the night's sky down to harvest little stars
into her naked body on their matrimonial bed.
her nipples in the mouth of god, she moaned a prayer:
what did i do wrong to deserve this man?
husbands are stained white bed sheets
she felt the warmth of her body in pillows.
marriage is a cult which sacrifices a woman's love
for a man's lust, she whispered to a dead man's ears.
maybe, just maybe, to love my husband faithfully
is to collect his blood drippings from the edge of the bed
into a white ceramic cup, mix it with pieces of brown papers
gulp the concoction and hit my breast three times.
no regrets! no regrets!! no regrets!!!
he is gone like yesterday. she laughed.

don't push it

you'd go back to her.
i've seen you eat back your love more often than you take coffee.
those were the words of another woman trying hard to
   convince a butterfly not to fly again
telling a bird the sky is too dangerous a city to roam about
dear, don't even touch the dial
simply, don't push it against the face of truth.
you prefer to sit on chairs in a relationship
you like to be folded like a dirty handkerchief
into a man's pocket. you love to hit the hard walls.
you love to be beaten into a small box
i prefer the dance floor
i like to laugh and cry whilst i watch the fires burn the rains
i love to hold hands and let go hands in the middle of strange nights
i love to see two adults enjoy their love
i choose the celebration of love, you choose the solace of confinements
i love to love, you love to be loved
you only celebrate love when it's coming from men
i respond to love no matter how it comes and who is bringing it
i guess you'd never know love if you fail to remember that
   we are still young;
and that we have too many dreams to go wild about
youth is wild. youth is not a period, but all the experiences
   you have in a period.
don't deny you the privilege of being young.
don't even try pushing love into a room without windows.
don't try to define it. don't. don't push it.

the thing around the waist of a woman

does your beauty scare you?
does your sexiness frighten your hips
from dancing to the tune of your name?

we have heard stories of women who held their beauties in
the eyes of men and rebuilt temples with a sway of their hips
of women who go on their knees at the rise of the first
moon to pray for a dwelling in their own bodies

we have learned all about hips.

and yet

we stare into your face, picking debris of your smiles from your cheeks
to design the contour of our own smiles,
waiting on your red lips to kiss us to death. men, we are.
lust in our waist, and love in our heads.

for bastards who knew more

are you going to run to shadows of the men in your body
because there's a gun in the hands of your bastard?
your son is so angry that he's giving up on tears
yet you gather bed sheets to cover your past,
to conceal the remains of their lust in your waist.
there's a reason why life is called life
and people alive can't even appreciate it.
are you naked? are your stretch marks wide enough like your womb?
run to the blue wall of your room
and instruct your son to put bullets to the beads around your waist
to set you free from yourself,
from everything that has defined you.
you're burning in your son's ungrateful eyes of fire and tears.

silent murderer

your husband fucks another woman.
he knows you know he is happy elsewhere.
he comes to bed with the guilt in his pants,
a long annoying face with a shameful stare at the clock
and a feeling of sympathy for you, yet you're still.

there's a voice in singing sands of deserts
that reminds you of your wedding vows,
of the holy kiss.
the same voice sings of how far you have come
to know infidelity is the murderer
who kills you slowly over years before you realize you're dead,
and yet you are still.
the white gown of the priest who officiated at your wedding
prompts you of how innocent your marriage was at birth
and quickly tears will from your eyes onto your flat breast
and when you remember what an adolescent your union
   has grown into.

each night you stare at jesus on the wall
and curse the day you were baptized.
you stand before a mirror
and yell: i'm beautiful. i'm alive, even though you know you're dead.

mrs grace nartey

a poem begins with a father who traded his children for riches.
some call it blood money. and ends with-
a woman in tattered jeans, almost naked
talking to herself. feeding on the debris of leftover foods
pausing to admire her long brown dreadlocks for several seconds
smiling at the frowning sky above her as if she saw jesus
as if it was her first time
hearing there's no god behind dark clouds
stopping traffic, ignoring the stubbornness
calling the taxi drivers long and funny names,
the drivers laughing and some almost annoyed, call her names too
passing kids stop to pick laughter or their legs from her gestures
wearing the air around her neck
and pieces of everything around her waist
supporting her nakedness with plastics
remembering that the love of her life ate yams from her womb,
and mentioning his name under the scorching sun
is her own way of seeking vengeance for her children
sitting briefly in silence, she counts her fingers
she is counting her children actually
trying very hard to remember their smiles, their hard faces
  against the concrete floor
their voices fading in a long echo with their
father's name
because her head becomes a vacuum
whenever the sun is at its meridian.
she wants to remember the colour of blood again,
but she smiles.
such woman is not called a mad woman
she is called a woman with a horn.

the streets of accra have a funny way of teaching people how to die
at the time when one is full of life

at first, they tell you the horns cannot be too heavy for the
   cow that must bear them
making you believe in things that don't exist
in yourself, believing in the abstract strength
to keep going even when you've no destination
to breathe even when you are down underwater
they say things like we are light, we pick each other up. we are light.
a woman believes and bears the horn
till she becomes the woman with the horn
eating waste and sleeping on concrete pavements of the streets
naming passers-by after her lost children's ghosts
and the male drivers, kwasi agyemang, the murderer of my
   kids, kwasi agyemang, my love. long and funny names.
memories have three ways of burying you alive: like the
streets of accra, memories instruct you to die
to live again on the third day
to die and live again like a mad woman.

erosion

a mother once said to her daughters
fill a man's heart with rich loamy soil
and plant in it a sprig of acacia
that it may blossom
but most importantly note that
the storm will pass by your garden
and manure will join the rest of earth
to be washed away.
away everything may
your sweet acacia may go to another woman
and strangely your acacia may be doing well
in its new earth.
dear daughters, verily! verily!! i say
acacias are not to be eaten
loamy soils are found in every pair of trousers
cry a short while for your lost acacia
refill, re-plant and expect the storm again
that's how to live loving a man.

leaving must mean l.e.a.v.i.n.g

i'm so tired of your presence
though you are gone
i still want you to go further away from here
there's a scent of you that lingers around me
it makes me shiver each night. i throw my hand in the air
and scream at ceilings 'please go, go to hell'

burn me. all of me in your possession
maybe that's how you set me free
maybe we both don't know how smoke
from burnt pictures and cloths ascend to freedom
maybe these naked children playing in the rain live in flames of fire.
please don't ever miss me, leaving must always mean leaving.

this stone you threw at me
has created a wound
too deep for time to heal.
this fear, i'm afraid is taking
the better side of me
this fear is taking the shape of your face
laughing at my jokes
while throwing white pillows at me
these memories of holding hands
are now nightmares.
you're hiding behind my closed eyes
and i always strangle you, almost dead
but i open my eyes to cough,
to search for breath, to never kill myself by suffocation
you've eaten all the air here. leave.

13 nights of sex before hell

do you believe in life after sex?
when we can't watch each others' face
and stare at our phones' screens.
do you believe i was the perfume in the air?
that which choked you. i laughed as you died.
do you mind if i shrink to the shape of a ship
and sail you from this fire to hell?

close your eyes and kiss my soul
pull me out of my body, out of muscles
and never think the sky is grey or blue
nor ever the wind carefree. we're all prisoners in this room.
if you did see a singer and a song in us
then it was because you were once an orchestra
until i changed the whites for the blacks on the piano
i don't love you, you don't love me. didn't we see it?

let me just push the world a little farther
to allow you more rooms to improve on your ego
or stab me in the back and taste me waste away
it is called soccer: you pass to who you know.
because no one celebrates narrow misses
so by all means score.

tomorrow is coming

you can stare at your wrist watch
and wish you were timeless and free to go.
but the wound in between your thighs
and the fading scar on your ring finger
very close to the remains of his love
will whisper your husband's name
at the time you decide to forgive yourself.
you'll realize a part of you had become the sea
without sands on its shores,
without the happy footprints of new lovers
and your wrist becomes the only enemy who whistles
to herald the second coming of christ.
you need water
you'll be thirstier tomorrow.

when she cums, she comes to her senses

when the world is inside the waist of a man
the universal language loses its meaning
in the ears of a woman who is waiting for a song,
waiting for a skin to wear and a shadow to represent.

ball by ball, she prays the rosary each night
kneeling before the cathedral in the man's pants
she confesses her only sin to god by moaning:
be gentle please, take it slow, don't push deeper
okay deeper, faster, faster, now slow, be rough.
chaos! chaos!! confusion! confusion!!

you have poetry stuck in your throat

you drank a calabash of dreams
with the aroma of sand
that mingled freely with the air
when the first drops of rain fell
from a bleeding sky to thirsty earth.
seated at the windows you were.
of the view was humid silence
of homeless birds who moaned
the ruin of their nests on a tree
and the wind they cursed to grave.

temporary everything in time
earth was gone with its perfume
in the ghostly wind that ripped
nature of its mystical content-
the nest and your dreams.
you imagined tomorrow today
from yesterday's labour
and tears eroded the life on your cheeks
as you measured the future of your marriage
in the recent dirges sang on the tree.

you have a poem in your throat
which begins with his name
and tastes like infidelity coiled
around cloudy fears of the end
and yet you could do nothing
but bathe in the ruins of rains
and re-frame your pains into gains.
you want to swallow his name down your throat
into the stomach. you swear to dump him in a shit.
that's all he has been, a bloody piece of shit.

smoke, words and cups

the day is a wild animal
in this chaos world,
and i don't want to die
at least, not again.
while the vapour from my white ceramic cup rises
with the innocent wind passing across
the length of my soul and beneath my troubled mind
i flip the pages of an old ritual book
with the hope of understanding happiness.
and of course, i would finally become a vapour too.
but i won't be living in a small cup.
i will from earth to the heavens.
i will stop briefly to mingle with the clouds.
and have the pleasure of telling
them about how humans made smoke
and continue my journey to the celestial,
sit at the right-hand side of him who created this day.
from thence, i will learn to be a smoke and a word,
a flower and its butterfly
a shadow without the owner
i'll gently learn to be nothing.

pride

she danced in the streets
the music reminded her of life.

she paid no mind to the men
who lurked around traffic lights.

she wrote, relaxed and drew
a shadow of how she would love
on a half broken mirror
and sighed and smiled.

stupid men in faded jeans
walking on the boulevard
lick my feet, she would say.

her hips were the music in the club
her delicate steps towards her end
she whispered to a man nodding his head
to her dance: lay with me tonight.

the dawn broke through her windows
to find her body motionless and lifeless.

mystical love

i was as sure as faith and dance
as darkness and its absence
and as heaven and humans.
i had no doubt god was here
and that god was there too
in sins, he was here and
in the holiest of holies, he was there.
it was a dark room under a dark rainy sky
with the stars hidden behind frowning clouds
it was the sound of percussion instrument playing
soft hymns to the atmosphere unseen
on the floor, seated we were:
legs crossed. right on left leg
right palm in left.
a black candle burned its wax away
to illuminate our dark life some ways
my husband had mastered his craft.
he wore a black cassock
he looked ahead of my head
and closed his grey eyes again softly.
he didn't want to breath.
i watched him dance to the heavens
head bent to the feet,
his waist curved around the dark,
hands thrown to the near west
heartbeats in accordance with every bit
of nature. it was with the rains on the roof.
i watched him turn into air and
back to a shadow on the wall
and i looked on with anxious surprise.
my lover finally became everything
i couldn't have been,
everything i had only dreamt of;

the moment
the air
he opened his eyes abruptly and
spoke to the silence and it broke
as above so below, he said and smiled.

why we are full of shit, women

finally, women, this poem promises to take us to where we began only to know the place for the first time.

we are natives of a nameless city, planted as hedges alongside the city's concrete boulevards.

we have many unnatural stories on our tongues to tell these natural men of lustful flesh and red blood, a lot more to scare them.

we are coming in our mothers' shoes and singing dirges in voices we stole from the faces of pages.

our mothers cooked their voices using their husbands' farts, so we're coming from the faeces of our fathers. that's why when we talk sometimes our husbands say we are full of shit.

there's lightning in the way we look at our husbands, thunder in our voices when we yawn and violent winds in our heads when we allow our chins to sink into our palms, but it is from the sky our husbands should expect the storm. because god is a disappointed wife of a womanizer too.

roman conversation

look beyond my glasses
what do you see?
well, a god said
he saw love wrapped in a brown paper.
and i laughed suspiciously.
i said my eyes remind me of my dying days
and he laughed even louder
and fell off the edge of the world.
i told him to remind me of why i love rome
before he becomes part of the air
which will finally break my lungs into dreams.
it's the only blessed and cursed city
you will ever know before you become a disappointed
goddess, he screamed aloud.
the echoes of his voice registered joy at my feet.
and i grew along the inner walls of a brown ceramic cup
with the froth of a hot cappuccino coffee.
i'll die but just not today, i responded.

no shame rapist

a happy old man had no name.
he responded to decayed whispers
that folded their arms in glorified silence
in his head.
mr. sinner, he whispered to himself
and he threw an elastic smile
which almost broke into a laughter
at the far ends of the world
and responded:
i know dead saints live
in flames of fire.
on a certain afternoon
when the world hid her shame
in droplets of rain,
the happy old man watched
the body of a girl in faded blue jeans
turn into colourful waters on concrete streets
and he whispered to himself:
youthful life like folded handkerchief
in the pocket of my room.
soon she will be victim before her own eyes.
like babies fondled the nipples of mothers
so did the happy old man laboured his waist
with friendly zeal and an infantile hope
for heaven to be same as hell.
when his industry came to west
like the twilight, he wiped the girl's tears and tasted it
salt-salty, he said and laughed.

how much is life?

i have often wondered how to die
that is if it was the best way to cry
wings if sold, i'd have bought to fly
i have seen tears descend on contoured faces
life without a whistle has offered me many races
i run too fast only to be the loser
i have many persons to blame, always a good accuser
life itself is not worth me
god or gods please let me be
or better deprive me of the chance to exist
if not so, then be calm while your commands i desist
sometimes i wish i could shout to quiet it all
and when it stops for a minute
i think about things that are minute
and when it gets better for a minute
i think about things that i really don't have to.
tell me
how much life is? i will buy one for myself.

be gone

sometimes i wonder how love will look like in tattered history books.
because history lives in a brown calabash full
of sour palm wine. and history dies in a 'shadowless' man
whose tattooed body is empty but has hands
to hold pieces of the history together.
i know why shy flowers bow their heads
before the cold morning dew
like how the smoothness of palm wine
teases a desirous long throat.
sometimes i think of how love will look like
in the eyes of my womanizer
when i finally break off.
i like to lie to myself, i say: he'll miss me when i'm gone.
i play too much in empty and dusty rooms,
sometimes i want to be serious for once
but i find myself in thoughts of how love
will have memories of me in history books.
i want to forget fashion,
forget religion
tear off my cloths
and step into history and be born again. be forgotten.

the power of the female skin

when a man returns to his own home like a thief
to steal the faces of his kids
begging for his presence
and pleading for his love for their mother,
there's a magic the woman can do:
lift the dark sky up
and search for god beneath it,
tell him a home
needs sunshine.
because there's sorcery on a woman's skin
which peels off the elastic cover
of heaven
and makes men see the nakedness of god.
it makes men appreciate for the first time that god is a female;
a woman is carefully crafted to represent sacredness.
her parts are delicate, she's a religion.

wells of our fathers

holes dug with beak of loves
papa worked hands of no gloves
rain and sun were no weather
days and nights were all days
papa worked with his self
digging this well of his blood
a water of blood to quench our future

earth to sky was no tall a tree
papa climbed and plucked the sun
erased the rainbow
collected the stars from the skies
and slapped the clouds
all to force down rains
to satisfy these wells

papa was brutalized
he was whipped by rods of tomorrow
he could cry out his sorrow
but he smiled for more lashes
all to make this future flashy

the depth of this well
he measured not
all he wanted was a well
dug!, dug!! and dug!!!
till he got lost in earth

where would we have been
if papa were you?
what would we have eaten
if papa had education and also wore suits?
what would have been our names
if papa had swallowed western norms?

today we carry on our lazy heads
buckets and pans of empty stomachs
fetching and drinking
red wines from the wells of our fathers
ignorant we are
that we drinking the blood of our fathers
from their own wells!

my son, i lied

i am a liar
death never made you fatherless
you are a four fathered son
all awake and working

you remember that story
which i narrated in tears?
it was not a fiction
i was the character
i was only a girl
i was a virgin

with my last breath
permit me to say
you are your family without me
you are your future without me
i am the victim of your make up
you are a product of my rape!

my lame friend

today i saw you in suit
wanted to say you look cute
but you were in an air-conditioned car
yet, i still could see your pain-scar

today, you had no helping boy
and so was filled with joy
valued added beggar
this afternoon you ate burger

destiny change-over
drives in range rover
gives lift to the market women
a good life omen.

minutes after, narrated your story
in no laughter, passengers said, 'oh glory'
i said, oh yes it was you
some years ago in your youth

crawling on your butts
making money by beggary but
you had a bachelor's degree
asked for my help and i agreed

wonder questions, how you did this?
how you left the street?
when did you buy a car?
how were you driving?
what job are you doing?

don't know when to get answers

i only know your old house, the street
nature shall bring us back
my old lame friend
glory be to god.

faustina ama dadson

whenever ama passed the street
she said a greeting in a voice sweet
the boys won't blink an eye to the flies
she was just as beautiful as blue skies

ama always carried a bag of books
a serious student with humble looks
and when she spoke, a courteous girl
her hair run down her butt in a curl

in fine, she had everything in herself
to make girls wonder about themselves
soon, they worked harder for the light
and went without the meat, and cursed the bread;
and faustina ama dadson, yesterday night
laid down the street bleeding dead.

hello mirror

people say we look alike
yesterday i fell, today i spike
but you mirror, why do you weep?
when you know tomorrow i reap
why is your heart hollering in red pains?
smile, the future holds our gains
i can see your bleeding eyes
afflictive cries in sleepless nights
with determination, away your worry flies.
hunted by the past
in your dreams, memories blast
fear cooks clouds in your head
raindrops of terror your nose shed
brighten up,
i see prof beneath your shame
i see a politician on top of the game
i see an engineer behind your chest
i see a writer and poet below your breast

i'm happy, mirror you smiling
are you me? or i'm you?
soliloquy.

nothing like a friend

in days of only sunshine without a shade
kill sorrow, sweat blood for it paid
when the night is yours alone without a kiss
stare at the stars but never a friend miss
don't let yourself sink
not even the ocean is deeper
because everybody cries but think
this friend doesn't see, day sleeper
paddle your canoe, never a helper
sometimes everything is wrong
clear your throat and sing a song
for no friend sells smiles or tears
so walk the miles without fears
everybody hurts
take comfort in yourself
iron your shirts
and dress neatly thyself
set a date with a mirror
talk, drink and smile clearer
and when you are angry with a friend
never throw a hand, just frown lend
it's just not worth your loneliness
try it, life is better with you alone.

when they say your best is not enough

chicks may throw their heads about in circles
they may flap their wings and fly to freedom
at the time freedom means the end of whatever is alive.
dead chicks are freed souls.

i say no matter how skilful chicks may be in a dance,
they will never please the hawk which hovers in the sky above them.

so my father said to me 'boy',
wearing a smile mixed with tobacco in his teeth,
'keep flying in styles, hawks are not the only judges in your sky.'

until you shine

step into an autumn garden
and make the leaves beneath your feet
play you these songs of persistence.

until you are great

dance so hard
as if you need to prove to yourself how good you are at dancing
dance
no one is watching you but dance anyway
dance
as though the earth owes you your past
dance.

it is fine to hide under a shade
while the sun is high

clementine and her john

are you lost in your reflection?
do you not find yourself in the mirror?
do you easily forget?
do you remember today is friday?
you and john pushed through bodies
to enter the red lighted hall
almost with laughter on your teeth
you kissed.
it was the beginning of something nice
until they came flying in the air
and froze everything that was alive
everything that could move on the dance floor
love became a crack in a sky
and john also became a doll in your arms,
life fading from his eyes as he calls your name
clementine, oh my clementine, save me
do you not remember some nights were too long
to fold into mornings?
no matter the sun in the sky, some worlds remain dark
like yours. like losing your lover on the night he proposed marriage.
clementine
oh! my clementine
save me
save me
save me, sweet clementine!
stand before mirrors
and try to discover that you are still beautiful
that it is a short life, that john went with only a part of you
that can be recreated, oh clementine, poor clementine.

about the author

Oppong Clifford Benjamin is a Ghanaian civil engineer by profession and an award-winning poet. His poems have appeared in *KWEE* magazine in Liberia, the *Portor Portor, Brittle Paper, WRR, Ghana Writes Literary Journal*, the *UK poetry library, BlogNostics, Vagabondcity Lit* and others. In 2013, *WRR Poetry* in Nigeria honoured Clifford as the Ghana Poet of the year. Clifford has read his poems in Ghana, Nigeria, South Africa, Germany, Rwanda and Russia. He has authored a collection of short stories titled *The Virgin Mother and other short stories*, published by Forte Publishing House in Monrovia, Liberia. Clifford is the founder of Ghana Writes Literary Group, the fastest growing literary company based in Accra, Ghana.

You can find more of his works at oppongcliffordbenjamin.com and ghwrites.com. You can follow him on Facebook: www.facebook/cliffordlabata; Instagram: @oppcliffben; and on Twitter: @glencliffben.

www.ingramcontent.com/pod-product-compliance
Lightning Source LLC
Chambersburg PA
CBHW030103100526
44591CB00008B/256